JESUS' PROMISES

A BIBLE DEMONSTRATION
IN VERSE

BY

ALAN SMITH

MOORLEY'S Print & Publishing

23 PARK ROAD, ILKESTON, DERBYS., DE7 5DA · ENGLAND

Each promise may be written on a card, or more effectively on the pages of a large "Bible", turned over before the passage of Scripture is read. (N.I.V.)

ISBN 0 86071 390 3

MOORLEY'S Print & Publishing

23 PARK ROAD, ILKESTON, DERBYS., DE7 5DA - ENGLAND

INTRODUCTION

God's Word is full of promises,
To us so freely given,
Of strength and peace and happiness,
And mansions bright in Heaven.
If we but take Him at His word,
Then we shall surely find -
His promises, they never fail,
For God is ever kind.
So let us read from God's own Book
These promises divine,
Where words of love on every page
In golden letters shine.

READING: Matthew 11:28-30

PROMISE NO 1:

"I WILL GIVE YOU REST"

To weary heavy-laden souls
These words the Saviour spoke;
There is no need for us to be
Bowed down beneath sin's yoke,
For He will give us perfect rest,
If we will just draw nigh.
This sinful world can never given
The peace for which we sigh.
He urges us to take to Him
The burdens that we bear:
His yoke is mild, His burden light,
And we find comfort there.

READING: Matthew 7:7-12

PROMISE NO. 2:

"SEEK AND YOU WILL FIND"

If in the goodness of the Lord
And His mercy we believe,
Whatever we ASK of Him in prayer
We surely shall receive.
Christ urges us to SEEK for Him,
He's waiting to be found;
And all who find the Saviour,
Their souls with joy abound.
He bids us KNOCK upon the door
That leads us into Life:
He ready stands to let us in
And shut out all our strife.

READING: Matthew 4: 18-22

PROMISE NO. 3:

"I WILL MAKE YOU FISHERS OF MEN"

The Lord chose humble fishermen,
Who answered at His call:
Disciples true they soon became,
For Him forsaking all.
And still today the Saviour calls
The humble, poor and weak;
We too may be His followers,
If all we will forsake.
We too, like Peter, James and John,
May serve our heavenly King,
And drawing in the Gospel-net,
A catch of souls may bring.

READING: Matthew 18:18-20

PROMISE NO. 4:

"THERE AM I IN THE MIDST"

Whenever His disciples meet,
Assembled in His Name,
The Lord's own presence in the midst
They rightfully may claim.
When we commune with Him in prayer
Though only two or three,
If we are all of one accord,
Then Jesus we shall see.
All worldly thoughts we must forget,
And, of one heart and mind,
Together join in mutual prayer,
Him in the midst to find.

READING: Acts 1:4-8

PROMISE NO. 5:

"YOU WILL RECEIVE POWER"

Endued with power from above
The Lord's disciples are;
And from the Day of Pentecost
They preach Christ near and far.
The nations must all learn of Him,
His Gospel all must know;
So when the Spirit dwells in us,
His power He will bestow.
Then we His witnesses become,
With power to proclaim
The glorious message of His grace,
Till all shall own His Name.

READING: Matthew 28:16-20

PROMISE NO. 6:

"I AM WITH YOU ALWAYS"

This lovely promise Jesus gives
To those in loneliness;
Our loved ones may be far away,
But Christ is there to bless.
He never leaves us comfortless,
No matter where we are,
But by His grace He helps us,
And keeps us in His care;
For He has given a Comforter
To strengthen and to guide,
And through His Holy Spirit
He's always by our side.

READING: John 14:1-6

PROMISE NO. 7:

"I GO TO PREPARE A PLACE FOR YOU"

The Lord has promised each of us
A blest abiding-place,
Where we with all the angel-host
Shall see Him face to face.
And now these mansions He prepares
For all those who are His,
That we may be with Him above
To share the heavenly bliss.
For, though 'tis heaven to be with Him
Upon this earth below,
When He receives us to Himself,
True glory we shall know.

PROMISE NO. 8:

"I WILL GIVE THEE A CROWN OF LIFE"

By faith the Christian overcomes
The world and all its sin,
Believing in the Son of God
A crown of life to win.
By faithfulness we all may claim
This promise of our Lord;
Though persecuted here below,
Yet great is our reward,
For when in Heaven we shall see
The King upon His throne,
Our crown of victory shall be
To hear those words: "Well done."

MOORLEY'S

are growing Publishers, adding several new titles to our list each year. We also undertake private publications and commissioned works.

Our range of publications
Includes: **Books of Verse**
Devotional Poetry
Recitations
Drama
Bible Plays
Sketches
Nativity Plays
Passiontide Plays
Easter Plays
Demonstrations
Resource Books
Assembly Material
Songs & Musicals
Children's Addresses
Prayers & Graces
Daily Readings
Books for Speakers
Activity Books
Quizzes
Puzzles
Painting Books
Daily Readings
Church Stationery
Notice Books
Cradle Rolls
Hymn Board Numbers

Please send a S.A.E. (approx 9" x 6") for the current catalogue or consult your local Christian Bookshop who should stock or be able to order our titles.